GARNISHING & DECORATING

Georg Hartung
Photographs by Thomas Schultze

Ideas for All Seasons

Schiffer Publishing Ltd®
4880 Lower Valley Road • Atglen, PA 19310

Other Schiffer Books by the Author:
Garnish and Decorating Made Easy, 978-0-7643-3932-5, $19.99

Other Schiffer Books on Related Subjects:
Creative Ideas for Garnishing & Decorating, 978-0-7643-3645-4, $19.99
Food Art: Garnishing Made Easy, 978-0-7643-1960-0, $19.99

Library of Congress Control Number: 2014938008

ISBN: 978-0-7643-4627-9
Printed in China

Published by Schiffer Publishing, Ltd.
4880 Lower Valley Road
Atglen, PA 19310
Phone: (610) 593-1777; Fax: (610) 593-2002
E-mail: Info@schifferbooks.com

For our complete selection of fine books on this and related subjects, please visit our website at www.schifferbooks.com. You may also write for a free catalog.

This book may be purchased from the publisher. Please try your bookstore first.

We are always looking for people to write books on new and related subjects. If you have an idea for a book, please contact us at proposals@schifferbooks.com.

Schiffer Publishing's titles are available at special discounts for bulk purchases for sales promotions or premiums. Special editions, including personalized covers, corporate imprints, and excerpts can be created in large quantities for special needs. For more information, contact the publisher.

This book was published 2013 © HEEL Verlag GmbH under its original title, *Garnieren & Verzieren: Ideen für alle Jahreszeiten*. Translated by Omicron.

Contents

12

28

Preface

Dear Readers,

Since my first book about the subject has been so successful and gathered positive reviews, I have been thinking about suggestions concerning the preparation and garnishing of small dishes and finger-foods, which would be interesting for hobby cooks, so this volume is all about preparing easy-to-do, delicious treats for your guests. For reasons of sustainability, I was particularly interested to show that the products presented here can be prepared seasonally. You may certainly choose to combine or arrange the small seasonal treats as a little buffet, but there is a good chance that you will use this book to refine some of your own creations to change their look. There are no limits to the imagination.

I would like to thank the photographer, Thomas Schultze, whose dedication, suggestions, and keen visual sense have greatly contributed to optimize the visual production of this book.

I hope that you will have a lot of fun while preparing these little treats and garnishings. Oh, and...bon appétit!

Georg Hartung

Tools

The joy of preparing food in a decorative way and the success of the cutting work depend on the skill of the chef, the quality of the food, and the functionality of the tools. Having good tools not only makes the job easier, but is a necessity — as there are shapes and effects that cannot be accomplished with a regular knife alone. For that reason, here is a brief overview of the most important tools and what they do:

The various shapes of **cookie cutters** are suited to cut-out fruits and vegetables, biscuit or sponge cakes, and gratins. These cut-out motifs are used for decorative purposes.

Just like with a pencil sharpener, radish, carrots, beetroots, pears, or turnip cabbage are passed through a **spiral cutter** and sharpened.

A **piping bag** with a star-shaped tip is perfect for making wonderful cream rosettes.

	A **sharp knife** is essential in every kitchen.
	Essential for working with fruits and vegetables: a sharp and handy **vegetable and fruit knife.**
	There is no quicker and more efficient way to rid a fruit of its skin than using a **peeler.**
	A **channel knife** is used to cut grooves into fruits and vegetables of different hardness.
	A **melon baller** (diameter between 3/8" to 1" or 10-30mm) is necessary to make balls and spheres out of fruits, vegetables, or butter. Its upper edge should be well sharpened.
	With the **Marzipan modeling tool** it is easy to make both simple and complex garnishments, and it also helps to shape a large variety of figures.
	A **skewer** is suitable to garnish and fix the most diverse food items.
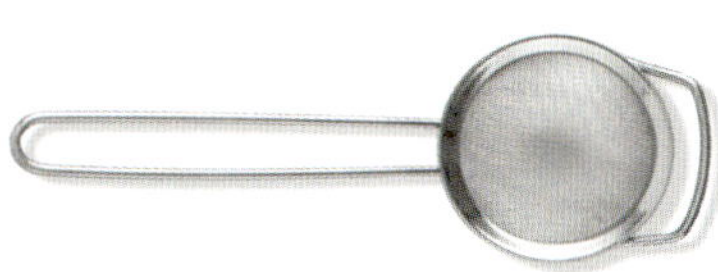	A **sieve** can be used to drain and strain food items, and help shape marzipan.

Making

1. Cut-out a small square from baking or parchment paper and then cut it diagonally with a sharp knife.

2. Roll up the triangle from the straight edge towards its center so that the longer part of the paper sticks out. Make sure that the paper cone ends in a tip.

Piping Bags

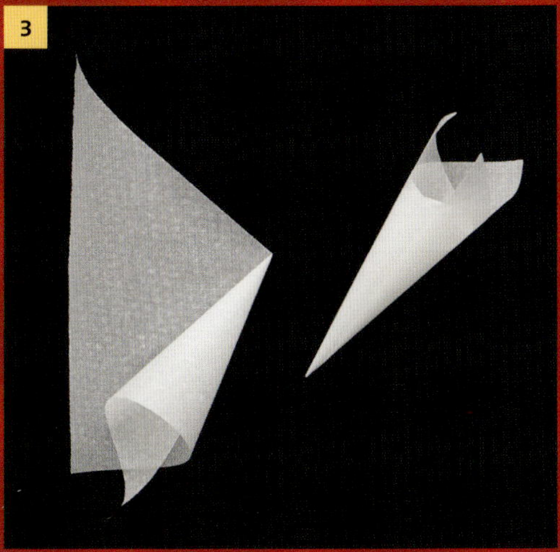

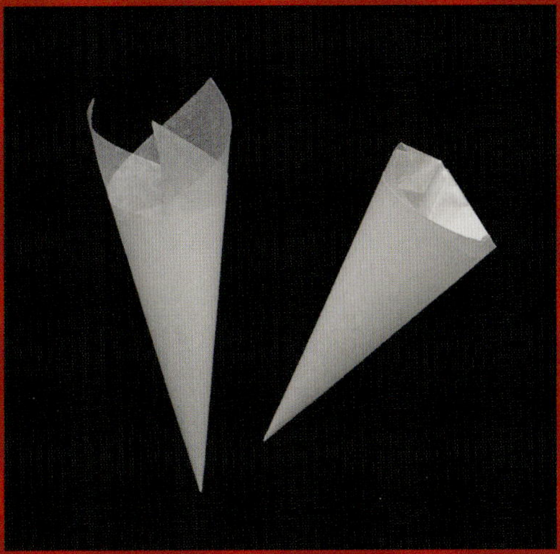

3. Flip the tip that sticks out towards the top and fold the rest of the paper into the small bag. You can adjust the tip before folding the excess paper into the bag.

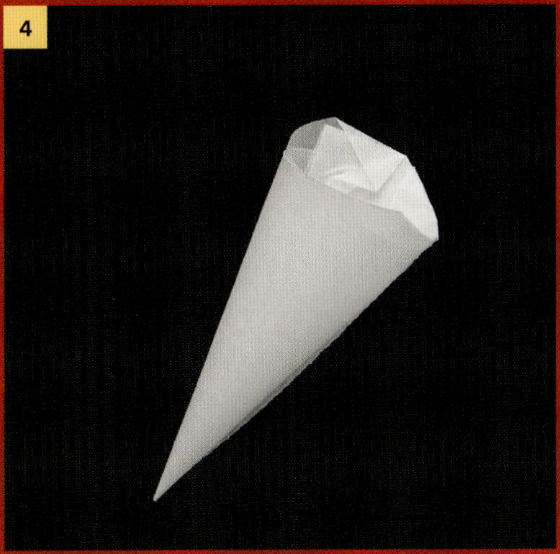

4. The piping bag for garnishing sauces and chocolate is now ready for use. It is also suitable for decorating marzipan figures.

Spring

Salad with Blossoms

INGREDIENTS:

Various kinds of leaf salad
Radish sprouts
Beetroot sprouts
Cocktail tomatoes
Various edible blossoms and flowers

For the Pumpkin Seed-Balsamic Vinegar Dressing:

1/4 cup (50ml) dark balsamic vinegar, about 5% acidity
1/4 cup (50ml) olive oil, cold-pressed
1/2 cup (100ml) canola oil, cold-pressed
20 pumpkin seeds, roasted
Small garlic clove, half
Salt and pepper, as desired
(optional) a little water

PREPARATION:

1. Thoroughly wash the leaf salads. Let them drip off and then cut them into strips. Place them into a bowl and decorate the salad with sprouts, cocktail tomatoes, and edible blossoms and flowers.
2. To prepare the pumpkin seed-balsamic vinegar dressing, combine the vinegar, the oils, the pumpkin seeds, and the spices, and put them into a tall jar. Stir the ingredients with an immersion blender to achieve a smooth dressing. In case the dressing turns out to be too thick, add a little water (1 to 2 tbsp. [20-30 ml]). Season with salt and pepper.

Onion Crowns with Carrot-Tomato Paste

8-10 pieces

INGREDIENTS:

1 medium-sized red onion, peeled
1/2 lb. (250g) carrots, peeled and finely diced
1-3/4 oz. (50g) tomato paste, triple-concentrated
3 tbsp. (20g) spring onions, finely diced
salt and pepper
ginger (powdered or fresh, finely cubed), as desired
honey, as desired
4 tsp. (20ml) oil
8-10 small red chili peppers
Cress

Additionally:

1 piping bag with star-shaped tip

PREPARATION:

1. Cut the onion at its center with a small knife in a zigzag pattern. Cut deep enough so as to be able to separate the two halves of the onion. You now have two onion stars.
2. Carefully pull the individual onion layers apart so as to make onion crowns. Briefly blanch them in hot water.
3. Glaze the carrots in a little oil and some honey for the carrot-tomato paste. Season with spices and honey and add 2 tablespoons (30ml) of water. Steam the carrots until they are soft, add the tomato concentrate and the spring onions, and blend. Season again with spices. Fill the piping bag with a star-shaped tip with the mix and pour into the blanched onion crowns.
4. Decorate the crowns with a small chili pepper and some cress.

TIP: If you want to serve the onion crowns as finger-food, make sure that they are quite small.

Carrot Swirl with Vegetable Filling

8 pieces

INGREDIENTS:

1-2 medium-sized carrots, peeled
1 small stem of leek
2-3 slices of pumpernickel (or any other bread)
Half a bunch of chives

For the Filling:

2 tbsp. (30g) pumpkin (Hokkaido), diced into very small cubes
2 tbsp. (30g) red bell pepper, diced into very small cubes
2 tbsp. (30g) carrot, diced into very small cubes
2 tbsp. (30g) green zucchini, diced into very small cubes
Salt and pepper
15 leaves of coriander, finely diced
1 tbsp. (20g) of honey
Half a clove of garlic, finely diced
2 tsp. (10ml) balsamic vinegar
4 tsp. (20ml) sunflower oil (or canola oil)

Additionally:

1 small knife
1 round cookie cutter of about 1-1/2" diameter (4cm)

PREPARATION:

1. Using a cutting machine, cut the carrot lengthwise into eight broad, very thin slices. Straighten the slices at the lateral sides using a knife. Cut the slices on one side at an angle, making these cuts close to each other. Briefly blanch the slices so they become flexible.
2. Peel eight thin strips lengthwise from the leek and blanch. Use one strip each to knot the carrot slices together.
3. Use the corer to cut eight small circles from the bread. Place one each of the rolled and blanched carrot slices onto the bread circle.
4. To prepare the filling, first fry the pumpkin, bell pepper, and carrot cubes in oil for about 2 minutes. Add the zucchini cubes. The vegetables should still have some bite. Season the vegetables with spices, honey, and garlic, and then add the balsamic vinegar.
5. Leave the vegetables to cool down a little, and then fill the carrot swirls with the vegetables. Decorate the carrot swirls with three shortened chives stems.

TIP: You can use alternative fillings, such as vegetable cream, liver cream, or others; fill by using a piping bag fitted with a star-shaped tip.

Carrot Flower

INGREDIENTS:

1 medium-sized carrot, peeled

Additionally:

1 small knife

1 vegetable sharpener

PREPARATION:

1. Straighten the edges of the carrot with a knife
2. Sharpen the carrot with the vegetable sharpener just like you would do with a pencil, making about 3-4 turns.
3. Unwind the long, curled carrot slice from the sharpener.
4. Fold the slice in such a way that the tighter section is at the center.
5. From the sharpened carrot, cut off the windings first and then the small, sharpened cone.
6. To finish the flower, place the rolled carrot slice onto the cone.

Spring Onion Grass

INGREDIENTS:

1 spring onion

PREPARATION:

1. Cut the spring onion in half and make several incisions at the lower section using a knife so that several "blades" are created.
2. Place the spring onion for about 15 minutes in some cold water. This causes the blades to curl and to look like grass.
3. Finish by cutting off the root.

Arrangement with Calla Blooms

1 arrangement with 3 blooms

INGREDIENTS:

1 fennel bulb
3 small red chili peppers
1 radish, peeled

Carrot Flower (page 20)
Onion Crowns (page 16)
Radish Cones (page 25)
Spring Onion Grass (page 21)

Additionally:
Several toothpicks

PREPARATION:

1. Cut the fennel bulb in half and carefully cut out the stalk.
2. Peel off the individual layers of the fennel bulb.
3. Now cut the fennel leaves so they look like calla blooms. Press one toothpick each from the top, downwards into the stems, and affix one small chili pepper to it.

4. To build the arrangement, take a 7-3/4" long (20cm) piece of radish and affix three calla blooms with toothpicks. Take care to put the calla vertically as they can tip over easily.
5. You can affix a carrot flower in front of the center bloom with a toothpick. Place two onion crowns in front or between the calla. You may put two radish cones next to the carrot flower. The gaps between the blooms are well-suited for spring onion grass so that the arrangements looks complete. Please affix all of the elements with toothpicks.

TIP: Smaller fennel bulbs are better for making an arrangement as they are easier to affix.

Radish Cones

INGREDIENTS:

3 radishes

TIP: Radish decorations look particularly nice with cheese and sausage platters.

PREPARATION:

1. Thoroughly wash the radishes without their stems and cut each one twice at one side, at its lower third, one cut below the other. Repeat this two more times so that you end up with three sides of the radish having been cut.
2. Place the radishes into cold water for some 15 minutes so that the cuts swell up a little.

Bell Pepper Basket

INGREDIENTS:

1 yellow bell pepper
1 cucumber (or 1 zucchini)

Carrot Flower (page 20)
Onion Star (see first step of Onion Crowns, page 16)
Radish Cones (page 25)
Spring Onion Grass (page 21)

PREPARATION:

1. Use a small knife to cut off the top of the bell pepper in a zigzag pattern. Remove the top and then remove the seeds and white sections inside of the pepper. Wash the bell pepper thoroughly. Even out the bottom of the bell pepper so it stands firmly.
2. Take a thoroughly washed piece of cucumber or zucchini and cut it so it will fit the width of the bell pepper. You will need it to attach the decorations and flowers.

3. Attach the carrot cone for the carrot flower to the center of the cucumber using a toothpick and place further toothpicks into the cucumber in order to attach more decorations.
4. Place the rolled-up carrot slice onto the carrot cone and put a red onion star and a radish cone onto the toothpick.
5. You can fill in the remaining gaps with spring onion grass.

Mother's Day Heart

INGREDIENTS:

6 egg yolks
3 egg whites
1/3 cup (70g) sugar
Pinch of salt
1/2 cup (60g) flour, sieved
2 tbsp. (15g) starch
Some butter for greasing
1/2 cup (150g) strawberry jam or currant jelly
1/2 lb. (300g) marzipan
3 tbsp. (50g) confectioner
1-3/4 cups (400g) whipping cream, beaten stiff
8-10 strawberries, cut in half
2 kiwis, peeled and sliced
2 tbsp. (25g) melted dark chocolate
4 cape gooseberries, cut in half

3 Marzipan Roses (page 78)

Additionally:

1 heart-shaped baking tin, about 9-2/5" diameter (24cm)
1 piping bag with star-shaped tip
1 wooden skewer
1 rolling pin
1 small piping bag (optional)

PREPARATION:

1. In two separate bowls, beat the egg yolk with the sugar and some salt until foamy, and the egg white until stiff. Slowly fold the egg yolk under the stiff egg white. In another bowl, carefully stir the sieved flour and starch using a wooden spoon and then fold under the egg mixture so as to achieve a smooth and even cake batter.
2. Place the heart-shaped baking tin onto a baking sheet covered with parchment paper. Pour the sponge cake batter into the greased heart-shaped baking tin. Make sure that your baking tin is even or the batter may seep out. You may fold the parchment papwer towards the top of the heart-shaped baking tin to avoid this.

TIP: In case you are short of time, you may simply buy two pastry or cake bases and use the heart-shaped tin to cut-out the hearts.

3. Pre-heat the oven and bake the sponge cake 10-12 minutes at 392ºF (200ºC). Use a wooden skewer to check whether the dough is done; the dough is ready when it does not stick to the skewer. Remove from the oven and let cool down.
4. Use a small knife to loosen the cold cake from its baking tin. Cut the cake heart crosswise at the center with a sharp knife. While doing so, keep rotating the cake and cut evenly towards its center so that the dough does not rip.
5. Coat the lower section with strawberry jam or black currant jelly. Place the top section onto it again.

6. Using a rolling pin, roll out the marzipan on your work surface. Make sure you use sufficient confectioner while rolling out the marzipan or it may stick to the rolling pin. Use a long confectioner palette to lift the marzipan base from the work surface. Use the heart-shaped baking tin to cut out a heart and place it onto the dough. Keep the marzipan scraps for later.
7. Place the heart onto a nice cake plate and decorate the outer edge with stiff whipped cream using a piping bag with a star-shaped tip. Make small rosettes along the top edge of the marzipan heart so that there are no gaps and no dough is visible.
8. Garnish the outer edge by alternating sliced strawberries and kiwis, which will stick to the cream.
9. Knead the marzipan scraps and roll them out again using confectioner. Cut two small strips of marzipan, one shorter than the other. Both should be of the same height. Use the melted chocolate in a piping bag (see page 10) to write “For” on the smaller strip and “Mom” on the larger one.
10. You can decorate the cake as you wish, e.g. using marzipan roses (see page 78) and sliced gooseberries.

NOTE: The cake should be consumed without much delay as the kiwis may turn bitter when combined with cream.

Summer

CHOCOLATE-COVERED FRUITS

MELON SHIPS

PANNA COTTA

VANILLA-RASPBERRY CUSTARD

PANNA COTTA WITH RASPBERRY MASH

GARNISHING SUGGESTION

CHOCOLATE ORNAMENTS

Chocolate-Covered Fruits

5-12 pieces

INGREDIENTS:

5-12 strawberries
5-12 cape gooseberries
5-12 grapes
1/4 lb. (100g) dark chocolate
1/4 lb.. (100g) white chocolate

TIP: It is easier to coat/cover the fruits if you use more chocolate and a deep receptacle.

PREPARATION:

1. Place the chopped white chocolate into a receptacle and heat to 104ºF (40ºC) over hot water. The receptacle should not touch the boiling water and be larger than the pot with the hot water. Make sure that no water gets onto the chocolate or it will become firm. While heating the chocolate, keep stirring using a wooden spoon.
2. Once the temperature has been reached and the chocolate has melted, cool it down quickly to 78ºF (26ºC). Heat the chocolate again to 82-86ºF (28-30ºC), using a candy thermometer to check the temperature.
3. The fruits can now be coated. They should be dipped only about two-thirds into the chocolate, so the fruit is still visible. This results in a nice contrast and keeps the fruit from being too sweet. Place the dipped fruits onto parchment paper and let the chocolate cool.
4. Proceed with the dark chocolate just as you did with the white chocolate. However, you need to heat up the dark chocolate to 122-131ºF (50-55ºC), cool down to 80ºF (27ºC), and then re-heat to 86-91ºF (30-33ºC).

TIP: You can serve the fruits on small, finger-food plates or a skewer, or place them in paper cups.

TIP: Melon ships make for a nice appetizer when combined with cold ham.

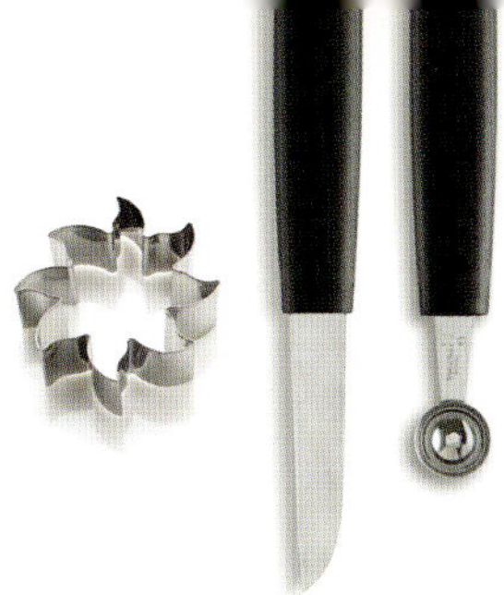

Melon Ships

INGREDIENTS:

1 Galia melon (or substitute with honeydew melon or cantelope)
1 pitahaya (or substitute with kiwi or fresh pears)
1 mango
A few clusters of black or red currant

Additionally:

1 small knife
1 melon baller, 3/4" diameter (2cm)
1 small star-shaped cookie cutter
1 machine cutter (or 1 long knife)

PREPARATION:

1. Cut the melon into large, half-moon shaped slices and remove the seeds. Use a knife to remove the fruit from its skin. Cut the melon ships four times so you end up with five pieces of melon.
2. Using the melon baller, cut-out several balls from a wide slice of pitahaya.
3. Using a machine cutter or long knife, cut slices of 3/4" (2cm) each from the mango and make small suns with a star-shaped cutter.
4. Place the mango suns onto the center of the melon ship sections and put the pitahaya balls on top of them.
5. You can add a nice contrast by placing one currant each on top of the balls.

Panna Cotta

5 servings

INGREDIENTS:

2 cups (500ml) heavy cream
3 tbsp. (40g) sugar
1 packet powdered gelatine
2-1/2 tsp. (12g) vanilla extract
1 vanilla pod, the scraped-out pith

PREPARATION:

1. Mix 1/2 cup (100ml) of the cream with the gelatine. Carefully dissolve the blend at about 176°F (80ºC). Add the remaining cream, sugar, vanilla extract, and the vanilla pod pith, and heat the mixture to about 122°F (50ºC).
2. Pour the cream froth into small glass bowls or small coffee cups and leave in the refrigerator to cool down.
3. If you want to overturn the Panna Cotta, briefly place the bowls or cups into hot water and put them on a plate.

Vanilla-Raspberry Custard

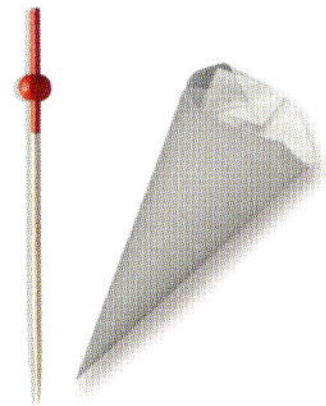

INGREDIENTS:
vanilla custard
Some raspberry mash

Additionally:
1 piping bag (see page 10)
1 toothpick (or small skewer)

PREPARATION:

1. Pour a long strip of vanilla custard onto a plate.
2. Fill the piping bag with the raspberry mash and place three evenly-spaced dots onto the vanilla custard. Using a toothpick or small skewer, trace each dot from top to bottom so that three small hearts are formed.

TIP: This custard is well-suited for desserts like Panna Cotta or Bavarian Cream.

Panna Cotta with Raspberry Mash

5 servings

INGREDIENTS:

Panna Cotta, for 5 servings (see page 38)
1 cup (200g) frozen raspberries
Powdered sugar, as desired
Half a lemon
1/2 cup (100g) heavy cream, whipped stiff
5 raspberries
1 kiwi

Additionally:

1 fine sieve
1 piping bag with star-shaped tip
5 glasses

PREPARATION:

1. Fill the glasses two-thirds with Panna Cotta.
2. Press the thawed raspberries through a fine sieve. Make sure you do not use the water resulting from the defrosting or the sauce might turn out to be too thin. Season the pit-less mash with some powdered sugar and a few drops of lemon. Cover the cooled-down cream with the raspberry mash.
3. Using the piping bag with star-shaped tip, garnish the dessert with one cream rosette each and then place one fresh raspberry and half a slice of kiwi on top.

Garnishing Suggestion

INGREDIENTS:

6 tbsp. (90g) vanilla custard
2 tbsp. (30g) fresh mango
Some raspberry mash
1 whipped cream rosette
1 chocolate ornament (see page 44)
1 mint leaf
1 black currant

Additionally:

1 small piping bag (see page 10)
1 toothpick (or small skewer)
1 piping bag with star-shaped tip

PREPARATION:

1. To prepare the mango-raspberry custard, mash the vanilla custard with the mango and pour the custard into a long strip onto the plate.
2. Fill the raspberry mash into the piping bag and place three evenly-spaced dots onto the vanilla custard. Using a toothpick or small skewer, trace each dot from top to bottom so that three small hearts are formed.
3. Decorate the Panna Cotta with a cream rosette using the piping bag with star-shaped tip, a chocolate ornament, a mint leaf, and one raspberry.

TIP: You can decorate the dessert with a marzipan rosette (see page 78) or other marzipan figures (see pages 72-80). A chocolate-covered strawberry (see page 34) is also well-suited for decorating this dessert.

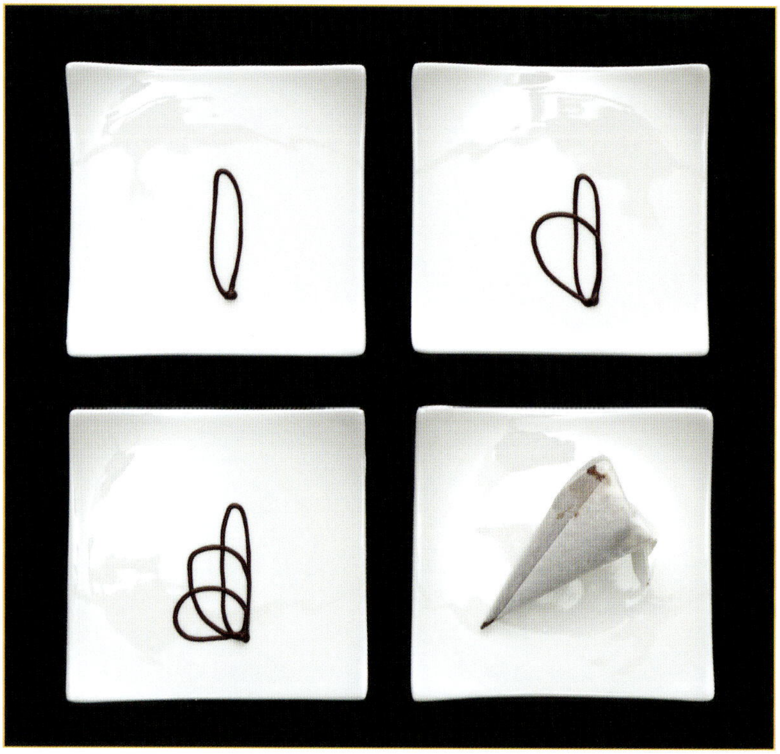

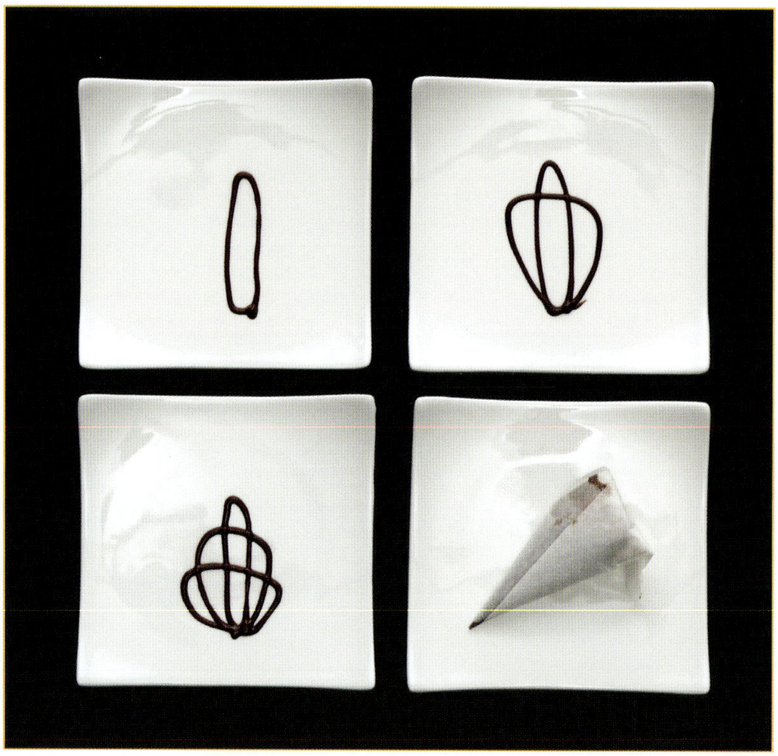

Chocolate Ornaments

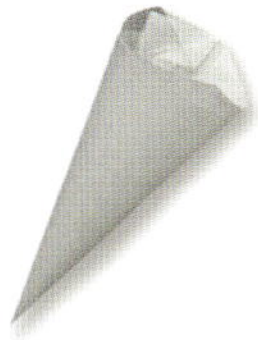

5 Chocolate Flowers or 12-14 Ornaments

INGREDIENTS:

For the chocolate flowers:
1/2 cup (15g) dark chocolate
1/4 cup (10g) raspberry mash
1/8 cup (7g) kiwi jam or jelly

For the ornaments:
1/2 cup (15g) dark chocolate

Additionally:
3 small piping bags (see page 10)
Parchment paper
Confectioner palette (or a knife)

PREPARATION:

1. You can use a base of parchment paper so that the ornaments are easier to remove later on. Always use a cold confectioner palette or a cold knife. The chocolate would melt if you were to use your fingers.
2. Using a small piping bag with melted chocolate (see page 34), draw a long oval onto the surface. Slightly below it, draw a bow and, below that, another one.
3. If you want to create a flower ornament, you must put the coating directly onto the dessert plate. Use the small piping bag to draw a flower of about 4" (10cm). Use new piping bags for the blooms and leaves by filling in the blooms with raspberry mash and kiwi jam or jelly for the leaves.

Autumn

STUFFED EGGS

SUSHI

WRAPPED SALMON ROLLS

BREADED COCONUT SCAMPI

MONKFISH MEDALLIONS WITH POTATO FLAKES

SCAMPI ON TOASTED BREAD

MOZZARELLA SKEWERS

Stuffed Eggs

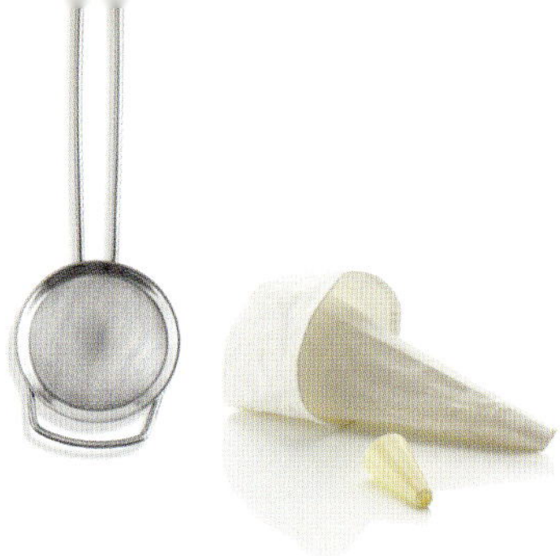

INGREDIENTS:
6 eggs
2/3 cup (150g) butter
Salt and pepper
Golden mustard, as desired

Additionally:
1 coarse sieve
1 eggbeater (or mixer)
1 piping bag with star-shaped tip

VARIATIONS:
2 tbsp. (30g) salmon puree
1 sprig of dill
1 teaspoon parsley, finely diced
1 teaspoon chives, cut into small rolls
1-2 chive stems
2 tbsp. (30g) chicken puree
1/4 bell pepper, finely diced
1 piece of cucumber
1 carrot

PREPARATION:

1. Hard-boil 6 eggs and place them into cold water. Peel the eggs and then cut them in half. Remove the boiled egg yolk and press through a coarse sieve. Mix the egg yolk and butter with an eggbeater and season with salt, pepper, and mustard.
2. Fill the egg mix into the piping bag with star-shaped tip and press it into the egg-white halves, creating a spiral shape.

VARIATIONS:

With salmon cream: Mix 4 tbsp. (60g) of the egg mixture with 2 tbsp. (30g) of salmon puree and fill the egg-white halves. Decorate the eggs with a bit of dill.

With herb filling: Mix 6 tbsp. (90g) of the egg mixture with diced parsley and chives and fill the egg-white halves. Decorate the eggs with short chives stems.

With chicken puree: Mix 4 tbsp. (60g) of the egg mixture with 2 tbsp. (30g) of chicken puree and fill the egg-white halves. Use finely-diced bell pepper as decoration.

TIP: To identify the various fillings, you can use cookie cutters, e.g., cut fish shapes from cucumbers or roosters from carrots.

TIP: You can also serve fresh fish, meat, or other vegetables.

Sushi

INGREDIENTS:

2 nori leaves
1/2 cup (150g) sushi or basmati rice, steamed
1 radish
2/3 cup (150ml) beetroot juice
1 kohlrabi
2 tbsp. (40-50ml) soy sauce

Additionally:

1 sushi mat (or plastic wrap)

PREPARATION:

1. Place a nori leaf onto a sushi mat. If you do not have one handy, then use plastic wrap.
2. Place the steamed rice onto the nori leaf. The rice should be lukewarm to be stickier.

3. Cut the radish and the kohlrabi into strips of about 3/8" (1cm). Steam the radish in beetroot juice while steaming the kohlrabi in water. Place the reddish-colored strips of radish at the edge of another nori leaf, then the white strips of kohlrabi, and then again the strips of radish. Cut the nori leaf so that the filling can be wrapped once.
4. Place the filling centered onto the first nori leaf.
5. Wrap the nori leaf from both sides around the filling. The vegetables should be at the center of the sushi roll.
6. Cut the sushi roll into several smaller rolls and serve with soy sauce.

TIP: Instead of using a nori leaf, you may cover the sushi roll with either black or white sesame seeds. You will need about 1-2 tbsp. (10-15g) per roll.

Wrapped Salmon Rolls

INGREDIENTS:

1 wheat wrap
2-3 tablespoons horseradish cream
2-3 leaves of lettuce (Lollo Bionda)
3-4 slices of smoked salmon
1 slice of lemon, quartered
1 piece of cucumber

Additionally:

4 small skewers
fish-shaped cookie cutter

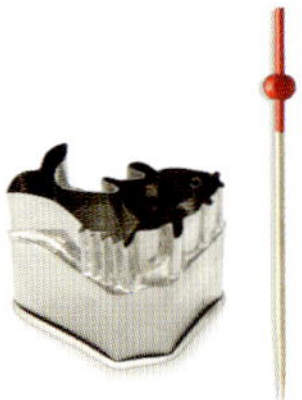

PREPARATION:

1. Spread the horseradish cream onto the wrap, and place the lettuce and then the smoked salmon onto the wrap.
2. Roll up the wrap as tightly as possible to avoid air pockets.
3. Place the lemon quarters on skewers and stick them into the wrap. Spaced them evenly so that the wrap will be held together.
4. To decorate, cut-out small fishes from the cucumber and place them onto the tip of the wooden skewers. Cut the wrap into small rolls.

Breaded Coconut Scampi

10 pieces

INGREDIENTS:

10 shrimp (fresh or frozen)
Salt and pepper
2 tbsp. (30g) flour
1 egg, whisked
3-1/2 tbsp. (50g) coconut flakes
1-1/3 tbsp. (20ml) sunflower oil
2 tsp. (10g) butter
1/2 cup (80g) mango, finely diced
4 tsp. (20g) pomegranate seeds

PREPARATION:

1. Season the shrimp with salt and pepper and dip them in flour. If you are using frozen shrimp, they need to be defrosted first. Turn the shrimp in the whisked egg and dip them in the coconut flakes.
2. Fry the shrimp on both sides at medium heat until they are golden-brown. Make sure that the coconut flakes do not get burned.
3. Serve the shrimp with small mango cubes and pomegranate seeds.

TIP: Instead of the mango-pomegranate seed mixture, you can also serve the shrimp with a sweet-and-sour sauce.

Monkfish Medallions with Potato Flakes

10 pieces

INGREDIENTS:

1-2 medium-sized potatoes, peeled
10-1/2 oz. (300g) monkfish filet
Salt and pepper
Oil for greasing
2 tbsp. (30ml) white wine

For the herb dip:

1/4 cup (60g) sour cream
3 tbsp. (40g) mayonnaise
2 tsp. (10g) dill, finely diced
2 tsp. (10g) chives, diced into rolls
2 tsp. (10g) parsley, finely diced
Salt and pepper, as desired
Medium-hot mustard, as desired

PREPARATION:

1. Cut the raw potato into thin slices and use a crinkled or melon baller to cut small circles of some 3/4" (2cm) diameter. You will need about nine potato circles for each medallion.
2. Cut the monkfish into ten 1-oz. (30g) pieces or medallions. Season with salt and pepper and place the cored potato circles onto them, overlapping with each other.
3. Place the monkfish medallions onto a greased baking tin. Pour 2 tbsp. (30ml) of white wine over them. Cook the fish for 8-10 minutes in an oven at 374ºF (190ºC). When the potato flakes take on a light brown color, the medallions are ready. To make sure they are cooked, press with your index finger onto the medallions. If they feel firm, you can remove them from the oven.
4. For the herb dip, mix all of the ingredients and stir thoroughly.
5. Place the medallions into a small bowl and serve them with the herb dip. Garnish with a bit of dill.

Scampi on Toasted Bread

INGREDIENTS:

1 slice of toasted bread
Some olive oil
1 small piece of butter
3 shrimp
1/4 cup (70g) horseradish
1/4 cup (30g) cranberries
Salt and pepper
Garlic, as desired
1 small leaf of lettuce (Lollo Bionda or some other variety)
1 slice of lemon, cut into three pieces
Some dill, finely diced

PREPARATION:

1. Cut the toasted bread into pieces of about 1-3/8" x 2-3/8" (3.5x6cm). Fry them with some olive oil and butter in a frying pan. Mix the horseradish and cranberries to make a sauce. Keep two of the cranberries for later. Cut the shrimp in half, and again transversely, and fry them with salt, pepper, and garlic.
2. Spread some sauce onto the toasted bread. Place a small salad leaf at the upper edge of the toast and put the cooled-down shrimp onto the rest of the toast. Remove the peel and skin from the lemon, as you only need the pulp.
3. Place one piece of lemon pulp and a cranberry between each shrimp. Finish by spreading some dill over it.

Mozzarella Skewers

7 pieces

INGREGIENTS:

7 cherry or cocktail tomatoes
3-4 basil leaves
7 mozzarella balls
Balsamic glaze, as desired

Spring Onion Grass (see page 21)

Additionally:

7 wooden skewers

PREPARATION:

1. Wash the cocktail tomatoes, cut them in half, and remove the stem. Place one slice of the tomatoes onto the skewers, then one mozzarella ball wrapped in half a leaf of basil, and then another tomato slice.
2. Place the mozzarella skewers "wildly" onto a white plate. Pour some balsamic glaze on them.

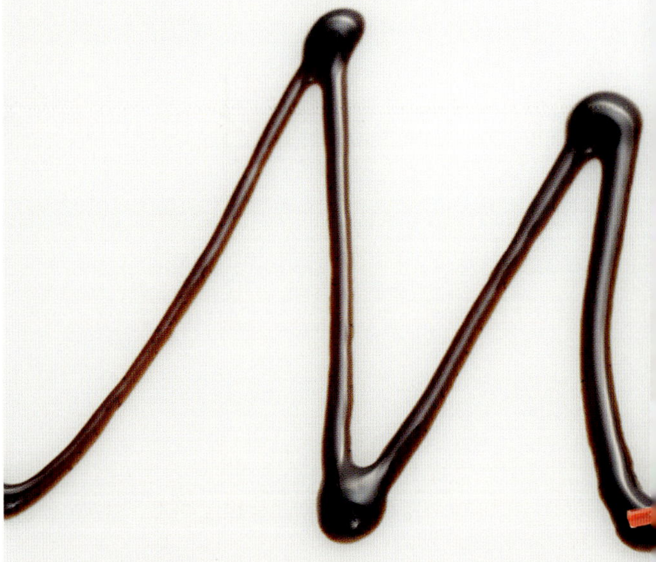

TIP: You can also arrange the mozzarella skewers into a circle, without the basil. If you do this, place some spring onion grass between them for decoration or place a mozzarella ball decorated with a ring of spring onion at the center. Finish by pouring some balsamic glaze onto the skewers.

Winter

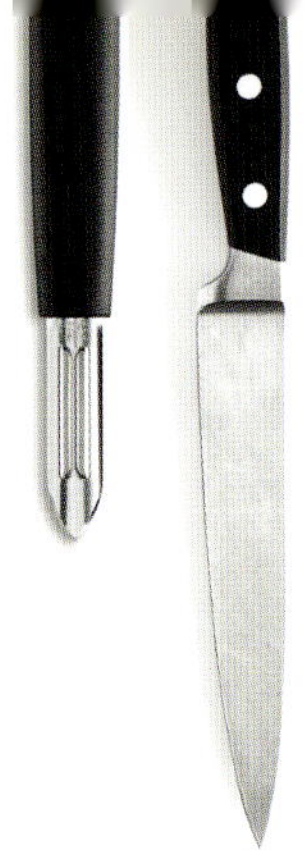

Potato Gratin Heart

10 servings

INGREDIENTS:

6 medium-sized potatoes
2/3 cup (150ml) milk
2/3 cup (150ml) cream
1 egg
Salt and pepper
Nutmeg, as desired
3-1/2 oz. (100g) Emmental cheese, grated
Butter for greasing

Decoration:

A few pomegranate seeds
Some chives

Additionally:

10 small heat-resistant ramekin dishes or moulds (about 5" long and 3" wide [13 and 8cm])
1 medium-sized knife
1 peeler
1 heart-shaped cookie cutter

TIP: You can also use a large baking tin and cut out several heart shapes from it.

PREPARATION:

1. Grease the heat-resistant moulds with butter. Cut the raw and peeled potatoes into very thin slices and place them into the moulds. Thoroughly mix and stir the milk, cream, egg, salt, pepper, and nutmeg. Pour as much of the mixture into the moulds until the potatoes are covered about two-thirds, and spread the grated cheese over the potatoes.
2. Pre-heat the oven to 356ºF (180ºC) and place the moulds inside for about 15 minutes until the gratin is golden-yellow.
3. Take the moulds from the oven and, using the cookie cutter, cut out ten hearts.
4. Decorate the hearts with a few pomegranate seeds and some chives.

TIP: You can also use grated beetroot as decoration.

Interesting Facts About Marzipan

Marzipan consists of finely-grated almonds and sugar. There are several commercial providers for fine marzipan paste. Make sure that the paste consists of at least 52 percent almonds. The higher the almond content, the better its quality.

The basic rule for using marzipan paste: the more humid the paste, the more confectioner needs to be added. You should always knead the marzipan paste with confectioner, as it makes it easier to mould later on. However, be careful not to add too much confectioner because the paste may rip. If you want to keep the prepared paste for later, cover it with plastic wrap — this keeps it from drying out — and store in a cool, dry place. If you spread the marzipan paste with a rolling pin, always put some confectioner on both sides. This will keep the paste from sticking to either the rolling pin or the surface you are working on. Surfaces such as granite, marble, and stainless steel, are best for rolling marzipan.

Marzipan paste can be dyed by using food coloring, either liquid or powdered, which can be dissolved with a few drops of water. When you color the marzipan paste, always mix the paste with the desired color and confectioner; the confectioner binds the humidity, so the marzipan paste is not too sticky, which is important when you work with it.

The marzipan figures shown in this book were created by first making a sphere, which was then moulded into its desired shape. In order to make several marzipan figures of the same size, weigh the marzipan paste sections carefully before making the figures.

Enjoy modeling and decorating your marzipan figures!

Marzipan Mouse

INGREDIENTS:
2 oz. (50g) marzipan
Some black food coloring
Some melted dark cholate for the eyes
Some melted white chocolate for the eyes

Additionally:
Moulding tool for marzipan
(or a Q-tip® with plastic wrap)
2 small piping bags (see page 10)

PREPARATION:

1. First make a sphere from the marzipan; shape it into a pear and put it on a plate.
2. Shape the tail with both hands and bend it slightly. Color a small amount of marzipan with black coloring and make a small ball for the nose. You can shape the ears like two small leaves (see Marzipan Rose, page 78).
3. Add the individual pieces (nose, ears, tail) to the body. Using the moulding tool or a Q-tip®, make two small indentations for the eyes below the ears. Take a small piping bag, fill it with melted white chocolate (see page 34), put some of it into the eyes, and let the chocolate harden. Another piping bag filled with melted dark chocolate is used to make the pupils on top of the white eyes.

Marzipan Piglet

INGREDIENTS:

2 oz. (50g) marzipan
Some red food coloring
Some melted dark chocolate for the eyes
Some melted white chocolate for the eyes

Additionally:

Moulding tool for marzipan
(or a Q-tip® with plastic wrap)
2 small piping bags (see page 10)

PREPARATION:

1. Color the marzipan with red food coloring and make a sphere. Shape it into a roll and make a snout using your thumb and index finger.
2. Using the moulding tool, make two grooves at the snout. Use the remaining marzipan paste to make two pointed ears and press them into the rear section of the head. Make two more small indentations for the eyes. Take a small piece of the red marzipan and make a longish section, and then twist it once to make a curly tail. Attach it to the rear part, centered on the marzipan figure.
3. Fill a small piping bag with melted white chocolate (see page 34), place some in the eyes, and let the chocolate harden. Fill another piping bag with melted dark chocolate to make the pupils on top of the white eyes.

Marzipan Hedgehog

INGREDIENTS:

3 oz. (75g) marzipan
Some black food coloring
Some melted dark chocolate for the eyes
Some melted white chocolate for the eyes

Additionally:

2 small piping bags (see page 10)
1 coarse sieve
moulding tool for marzipan
(or a Q-tip® with cling wrap)

PREPARATION:

1. Take half of the marzipan and color it black, and then press it through a coarse sieve (for the spines). Make a small ball for the nose as well.
2. Take the remaining marzipan and make a pear. Place it flat onto a plate and attach the spines to the wide body section. Press the nose onto the tip of the head.
3. Using the moulding tool or Q-tip®, make the grooves for the eyes. Fill a small piping bag with melted white chocolate (see page 34) and put some of it into the eyes; let the chocolate harden. Fill another piping bag with melted dark chocolate is to make the pupils on top of the white eyes.
4. Using the melted dark chocolate, paint the whiskers next to the eyes and the mouth under the nose.

Marzipan Rose

INGREDIENTS:

1/2 oz. (13g) marzipan
Some red food coloring
Some green food coloring

PREPARATION:

1. Take 2/3 of the of marzipan and color it red; color the other 1/3 green. Using the green marzipan, make three slightly large and pointed leaves. Now, make several leaves of varying size from the red marzipan. Roll up a small red leaf for the center of the rose. Take three of the larger red leaves, press them onto each other to make the flower, and then add five even larger red leaves around the bud.
2. Finish by adding three green leaves below the flower.

Marzipan Snowman

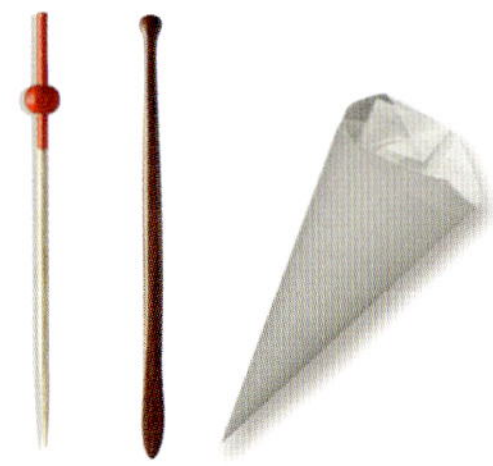

INGREDIENTS:

4 oz. (112g) marzipan
Some black, red, green, and orange food coloring
Some melted dark chocolate for the eyes
Some melted white chocolate for the eyes

Additionally:

2 small piping bags (see page 10)
Toothpicks (optional)
Modeling tool for marzipan
(or a Q-tip® with plastic wrap)

PREPARATION:

1. Use 3/4 of marzipan to make a large, medium, and small sphere and two arms for the snowman.
2. Now, take a small amount of marzipan, color it black, and use it to make a small cone for the hat, as well as a small, flat piece. Put both of them together. Make five small balls for the buttons.
3. Taking an even smaller amount of marzipan, color it orange and shape it into a small cone for the nose.
4. Color the remaining marzipan red and green. Form two "sausages" from each one and twist them around each other to obtain a two-colored scarf.

5. Assemble the snowman: from bottom to top, first the large sphere, then the medium sphere, and then the small sphere. Attach the arms at the top section of the medium sphere. Place the hat on top and wrap the scarf around its neck. Attach the black buttons to the body, one below the other. Now, attach the nose; use a toothpick in case it does not stick to the head.
6. Using the moulding tool or Q-tip®, make the grooves for the eyes. Fill a small piping bag with melted white chocolate (see page 34) and put some of it into the eyes; let the chocolate harden. Fill the other piping bag with melted dark chocolate to make the pupils on top of the white eyes.

Dark Chocolate Mousse

For 40 finger-food spoons

INGREDIENTS:

7 oz. (200g) fine dark chocolate
4 tbsp. (60ml) espresso
5 egg yolks
2 tbsp. (30g) vanilla extract
1/2 cup (125g) cream, whipped
5 egg whites, whipped
3-1/2 tbsp. (50g) sugar
20 gooseberries
40 mint leaves

Additionally:

1 piping bag with star-shaped tip
40 finger-food spoons

PREPARATION:

1. Melt the chocolate (see page 34) and add the espresso. Stir the egg yolks and vanilla extract into a froth and add the mix to the chocolate. Using a wooden spoon, carefully fold in the whipped cream and then the whipped egg white and sugar.
2. Fill the piping bag with the mixture and press onto the finger-food spoons to make a spiral.
3. Decorate each spoon with half a gooseberry and a mint leaf.

TIP: You can vary the chocolate mousse with some ground cinnamon, as well as rum, Cointreau®, or other liquors.

White Chocolate Mousse

For 20 finger-food spoons

INGREDIENTS:

3 egg yolks
4 tbsp. (60g) sugar
1/2 cup (125g) white chocolate
2 tsp. (10ml) rum
3 tbsp. (40g) butter
2 tsp. (10ml) water
2 gelatine packets
3 egg whites
1/2 cup (125g) cream, whipped
Kiwi, peeled and sliced thin
A few panicles/clusters of black or red currant

Additionally:

20 finger-food spoons
1 piping bag with star-shaped tip

PREPARATION:

1. Stir the egg yolks and 2-1/2 tbsp. (30g) of sugar into a froth so that the sugar dissolves. Melt the chocolate (see page 34) and combine with the egg yolk-sugar mixture.
2. Stir the rum, butter, and water, dissolve the gelatine, and mix directly with the egg yolk-sugar and cholate mixture.
3. Whip the egg white and 2-1/2 tbsp. (30g) of sugar until stiff and carefully fold into the mixture. Now, fold the whipped cream into the mixture.
4. Put the chocolate mousse in the refrigerator for 2-3 hours.
5. Fill the piping bag with the mousse and press onto the spoons, making a spiral. Decorate each spoon with a black or red currant and a piece of kiwi.

Semolina Flummery Confections

30-35 pieces

INGREDIENTS:

1 cup (250ml) milk
1 pinch of salt
5 tsp. (25g) sugar
3-1/2 tbsp. (50g) hard or durum wheat semolina
1 egg yolk
1/4 vanilla pod, the scraped-out pith
2 tsp. (10ml) Grand Marnier®
1/3 cup (70g) cottage cheese, 40% fat content
5-1/2 tbsp. (80g) almond flakes, roasted
A few panicles/clusters of black or red currant

Additionally:
Paper cups

PREPARATION:

1. Boil the milk with salt and sugar. Pour in the semolina and boil again while stirring and then let soak for about 5 minutes.
2. Add the egg yolk, vanilla pith, and Grand Marnier and stir together. Add the cottage cheese and stir together again. Let the mixture cool down. Meanwhile, briefly roast the almond flakes.
3. Make balls from the mixture so that they fit into paper cups and dip them in the roasted almond flakes.
4. Place the confections into the paper cups and garnish with one black or red currant each.

TIP: Instead of currants, you may use other fruits such as raspberries or gooseberries.